With Compliments from the Manufacturer ...

ActHIB®
Haemophilus b Conjugate Vaccine
(Tetanus Toxoid Conjugate)

Tripedia®
Diphtheria and Tetanus Toxoids and
Acellular Pertussis Vaccine Adsorbed

TriHIBit®
ActHIB® Haemophilus b Conjugate Vaccine
(Tetanus Toxoid Conjugate) reconstituted with
Tripedia® (Diphtheria and Tetanus Toxoids and
Acellular Pertussis Vaccine Adsorbed)

101 Ways
To Know If You're A
Nurse

by Neil Shulman, M.D.
Illustrations by Kristin Anlage

ISBN: 1-892157-00-4

Published by RX HUMOR
2272 Vistamont Dr., Decatur, GA 30033

Text copyright, 1998 by Neil Shulman
Illustrations by Kristin Anlage
Graphic Design by Relevant Vision

Printed in USA
Library of Congress Number 98-066220
ISBN: 1-892157-00-4

DEDICATION

To the nurses of the world who bring a special dimension to health care.

An extra special thanks to mom and dad, who have an infectious sense of humor which they have encouraged me to carry throughout my career.

ACKNOWLEDGMENTS

Thanks to Robin Voss, for her invaluable assistance and insight.

1. Your children are accustomed to having their vital signs checked in the middle of the night.

2. You water the ivy in your front yard with D5W.

3. You call poison control when your kids get hiccups at the dinner table.

4. You use white panty hose for
your Christmas stocking.

5. You've actually seen doctor's orders in your two-year-old's scribbling.

6. You have difficulty resisting the urge to pump the chest of anyone who kisses you on the mouth.

7. You either wake up very early,
go to bed very late, or don't sleep at night.

8. You re-evaluate your cat's prescription medicine
from human doses and then
call your favorite rep for a free sample.

9. All your children have emergency buzzers
by their bedsides.

10. You know the white cap is a geriatric thing.

11. You answer the phone at home with,
"Can I help you?"

12. You hug friends in the Heimlich position.

13. Your family is growing tired of your correcting doctor's orders while they're trying to watch "ER" and "Chicago Hope."

14. You make your spouse sign out aspirin from the medicine cabinet.

15. You feel like your checkbook balance column should be titled LTC.

16. Your neighbors save far too much money on medical advice.

17. You check for good veins every time
you shake someone's hand.

18. The conversations at your dinner parties revolve around bodily fluids.

19. You would be very wealthy if paid
one dollar each time a friend asks,
"What does it mean when this happens?"

20. Patients ask you all of the important questions after the doctor leaves the room.

21. You maintain detailed charts of all your arguments with your mother-in-law.

22. You wear safety glasses and Latex™ gloves when treating your children's cuts.

23. Doctors don't intimidate you,
they just make you smile and
grit your teeth.

24. You bring salad dressing for lunch
in urine specimen cups.

25. All the televisions in your home
are mounted curiously high.

26. You're smart enough to not be a doctor.

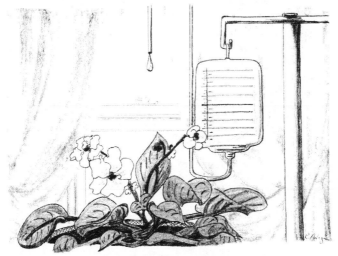

27. You use tube feeding bags to drip water into your plants when you're on vacation.

28. Your kids know to expect respiratory isolation when they catch a cold.

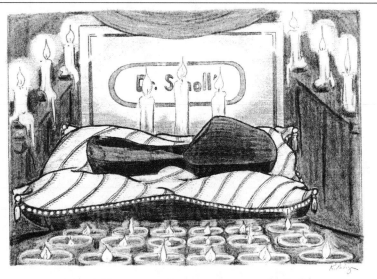

29. *All* your shoes are sensible.

30. You hate the word "impaction."

31. You yell "knife" and slap it in your spouse's hand to carve the Thanksgiving turkey.

32. You've discovered that bedpans make excellent chip-and-dip trays.

33. You're the only person on the block with a sterilizer in the kitchen.

34. All of your sleepwear is
    stolen property from
    the hospital operating room.

35. You always celebrate holidays
a day late or a day early.

36. On your off days, you make your family stay up with you until 7 a.m. just so you don't get off schedule.

37. You keep charts on your kids.

38. You've seriously thought of catheterizing your children before taking them on long car trips.

39. You use TPN to fertilize shrubs and flowers.

40. Soap opera nurses unnerve you.

41. Your sister doesn't understand why you always look at her ankles when she's short of breath.

42. You wear isolation gowns when you cook.

43. You see a doctor more than anyone
would want to.

44. You've embarrassed dinner dates as you sterilized restaurant utensils using a candle and a glass of water.

45. You can't become romantically involved
without first performing a complete checkup.

46. You have an enormous bladder.

47. You are sometimes home for a couple of hours before you remember that it's okay to sit down.

48. Everything in your laundry basket is folded with hospital corners.

49. You realize that the "crisp white" days have passed.

50. You are among the proud few who make a legal living pushing drugs all day.

51. All your dishes have covers.

52. You don't feel guilty
finding humor in
horrible situations.

53. All your friends are either pharmacists, nurses, doctors or patients.

54. You tend to collect a mid-stream sample
every time you go to the bathroom.

55. You think misbehaving children merit leather restraints.

56. You fantasize about having your mother-in-law
sign a DNR when she comes to visit.

57. Your spouse's handwriting reminds you of ventricular fibrillation.

58. Your children know they never want to be a nurse.

59. You get even with your family via mechanical diets.

60. You can't believe nurses really used to stand when a doctor entered the room.

61. You've designed your kitchen
after a nurse's station.

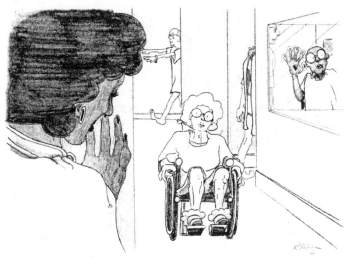

62. Senile old men and women tend
to gravitate toward you.

63. Your shot glasses at home are graduated in mls.

64. You call bedtime the "change of shift report."

65. You get perverse pleasure out of calling doctors in the middle of the night.

66. You know how to rephrase a diagnosis so that it sounds like the doctor's idea.

67. You've developed an uncanny knack for making doctors feel important.

68. You wish the guy behind the deli counter
wouldn't yell "number 99!"

69. You firmly believe that annoying spouses should be sedated.

70. The coat rack in your home looks
suspiciously like an IV pole.

71. You catch yourself laying out your makeup
on a tissue like a surgical prep.

72. You meet friends at 1500, not 3:00.

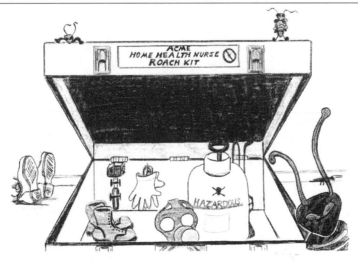

73. You know about the
home-health-nurse-cockroach-dance.

74. You obsess over bowel movements
and color of sputum.

75. You give your patients secret nicknames.

76. You use your stethoscope to eavesdrop
on next-room conversations.

77. Even your guest soaps are antibacterial.

78. You wrap presents with surgical tape.

79. Your kids have water balloon fights
with surgical gloves.

80. You've discovered that medicine cups, tongue depressors and rolls of Curlex® gauze make excellent stand-ins for Christmas bells, candy canes and tinsel.

81. You look for chest movement in any sleeping person.

82. You make Jell-O® shooters in medicine cups.

83. You've said, "gimme a break" at least six times while watching reruns of "Marcus Welby, MD."

84. While on the cereal aisle, you diagnose
medical syndromes of passing shoppers.

85. Your son-in-law doesn't understand why your daughter still insists on "mitering the corners" of all her sheets.

86. You have accepted varicose veins
and swollen ankles as a fact of life.

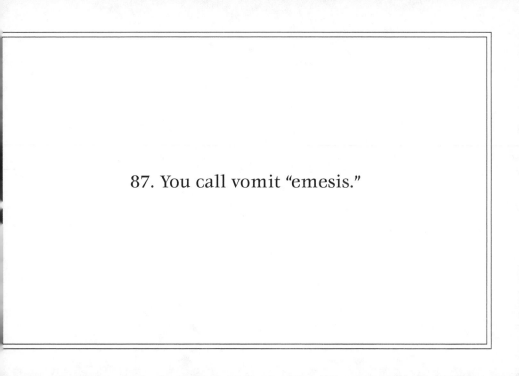

87. You call vomit "emesis."

88. Your cooking-utensil drawer contains
at least one syringe.

89. You and your friends have turned out-goring each other into an Olympic sport.

90. Your blood pressure hardly responds to
being cursed out by a doctor.

91. You know anyone claiming to be a nurse but wearing a watch with no second hand is a fraud.

92. You think other parents are awfully ignorant to let their children get gas by drinking out of a straw.

93. You go to sleep dreaming about
I and Os and lab values.

94. You suppress fantasies of assisting Dr. Kervorkian.

95. You haven't been invited back to a dinner party since the last time you gave a detailed description of a patient's perforated appendix over dessert and coffee.

96. You're the only one in your aerobics class using a urinal as a water bottle.

97. You've received at least one decorated scrub jacket for Christmas.

98. You've seen so much nudity that
"BayWatch" doesn't begin to turn you on.

99. You look for errors in your children's anatomically correct dolls.

100. You store your mother-in-law's leftover meals in red biohazardous garbage bags.

101. Your friends never want for pharmaceutical pens, mugs or pads of paper.

About Neil Shulman, M.D....

Neil's comic personality has launched him into a successful career in entertainment where he has been using humor as therapy in a unique one-man traveling comedy show. Favorable reviews and publicity—from CNN, *U.S.A. Today, The Miami Herald*—keep him booked before many audiences, from comedy clubs and colleges to national conferences to a United Nations peace mission in Cyprus. He philosophizes, performs monologues and tells of comic adventure, mixing the worlds of medicine, movies and novels.

Shulman wrote the book Doc Hollywood, then co-produced the Michael J. Fox-starring motion picture his book inspired. Shulman's other fiction includes *The Backyard Tribe, Finally...I'm a Doctor, Life Before Sex, What's in a Doctor's Bag?, Under the Backyard Sky* and *Second Wind.*

For speaking engagements, Shulman may be reached at (404) 321-0126, 2272 Vistamont Drive, Decatur, GA, 30033, nshulman@emory.edu or www.dochollywood.com

OTHER BOOKS AND VIDEOS BY NEIL SHULMAN

Fiction
The Backyard Tribe
Doc Hollywood
Finally...I'm a Doctor
Life Before Sex
Second Wind
What? Dead...Again?

Children's Books
The Germ Patrol
Under the Backyard Sky
What's in a Doctor's Bag?

Non-Fiction
Better Health Care for Less
The Black Man's Guide to Good Health
High Blood Pressure
Let's Play Doctor
Understanding Growth Hormone

Videos
The Real Doc Hollywood Unlocks the Mysteries of Hollywood

What's in a Doctor's Bag?

MKT4788